T0208899

WAKE
UP!

How to Invigorate Your Faith
in an Apathetic Culture

Emily DeRienzo

WESTBOW
PRESS®
A DIVISION OF THOMAS NELSON
& ZONDERVAN

WestBow Press books may be ordered through booksellers or by contacting:

WestBow Press
A Division of Thomas Nelson & Zondervan
1663 Liberty Drive
Bloomington, IN 47403
www.westbowpress.com
1 (866) 928-1240

ISBN: 978-1-9736-8439-8 (sc)
ISBN: 978-1-9736-8438-1 (e)

Library of Congress Control Number: 2020901415

Print information available on the last page.

WestBow Press rev. date: 2/21/2020

To my Lord and Savior Jesus Christ,

Who has called me to write this book for His glory.

CONTENTS

A NOTE TO THE READER

On the first day of the week we came together to break bread. Paul spoke to the people and, because he intended to leave the next day, kept on talking until midnight. There were many lamps in the upstairs room where we were meeting. Seated in a window was a young man named Eutychus, who was sinking into a deep sleep as Paul talked on and on. When he was sound asleep, he fell to the ground from the third story and was picked up dead. Paul went down, threw himself on the young man and put his arms around him. "Don't be alarmed," he said. "He's alive!" Then he went upstairs again and broke bread and ate. After talking until daylight, he left. The people took the young man home alive and were greatly comforted.

—Acts 20:7–12

All throughout the Bible, stories of heroes, villains, God, Satan, and more unfold to tell the story of humanity and God's ultimate plan of love. Some stories are less popular than others, yet they carry extremely important messages that everyone needs to hear. Such a story is found in Acts

20:7–12. Not many people are familiar with this portion of the Bible, and that is exactly why I wrote this book. Every word of the Bible is vital to God's story, including this portion from Acts that I have chosen to write about. *Wake Up* helps you find truths of the Christian faith that burst out from the pages of the Bible and aid you in navigating through this seemingly unimportant story. I also want to note that I designed this book to have principles within each chapter that build upon one another to help mature your faith and strengthen your walk with God. God inspired me with this writing, and I prayed for guidance every time I placed words in this book. Additionally, I have prayed over you specifically, the reader of this book, and have asked God to reveal Himself to you and transform your life through His Word. It may not be difficult to read the ink on the following pages, but it will be a challenge to take to heart and put into action what it says. I encourage you to pray for enlightenment while you read this book and strive to live out the following principles in your day-to-day life. "The Lord bless you and keep you; the Lord make his face shine on you and be gracious to you; the Lord turn his face toward you and give you peace" (Numbers 6:24–26).

In Christ,
Emily DeRienzo

CHAPTER 1

Fellowship

On the first day of the week we came
together to break bread.

—Acts 20:7

Let me set the stage for the story we will be examining. I want you to imagine a multistory home illuminated by candlelight. It is late at night, and people silently enter the building and make their way up to the third floor. Upon entering the room, Paul (the apostle) is seen preaching to the people, while the early Christians are sharing with one another and praising God in unison. These Christians are fellowshipping—spending time with God and with one another. Paul had a lot to say about fellowship; however, earlier accounts of fellowship are recorded in the Old Testament.

We can go all the way back to the story of creation. God created the world in seven days. On day six, God created humans. Adam was the name of the first human being God made, and Adam was made in His image. After breathing life into him, God tasked Adam with caring for all He had created on the previous days. Despite the vast array of animals additionally created on the sixth day, Adam still felt alone. He searched for a "suitable helper," but "no suitable helper was found" (Genesis 2:20). Adam was at a loss. He longed for companionship. Adam was desperately searching for another person—someone to be with, to share his life with, and to enjoy God with. No animal was suitable, so what could Adam do?

This circumstance demonstrates that Adam couldn't do anything using his own power. In fact, the only thing he was able to do (search for a mate) failed. God cares about our relationships so much so that He said, "It is not good for the man to be alone. I will make a helper suitable for him" (Genesis 2:18). Not only does God acknowledge man's need for a helper, but He wants to give him the gift of community. God aided Adam in giving him exactly what he needed. God created Eve. A woman. A human. This is God's plan for Christians: to "encourage one another and build each other up" (1 Thessalonians 5:11). We are supposed to walk with God together and invigorate one another to continue in our faith. Adam and Eve literally walked with God. Throughout the rest of the Bible, we observe how God walks with those who choose to follow Him.

Before we look at how this concept relates to our story of interest, I want you to imagine a battlefield. Think of green grass stretching for miles, rocky cliffs surrounding the field, and millions of warriors on one side. On the other side, place another million warriors. Imagine the outcome, assuming both sides are equally trained and equipped. Now remove all men from one side but one single warrior, and keep the million on the other side. Not a pretty outcome for the single warrior. Now shrink back the opposing army to one thousand, then to one hundred, and finally to ten. Even with only ten men against the one, he likely would still lose. This is the same for Christians. When hardships come, and they will, Satan rears up his army. His mission is to pull us as far away from God as possible. Satan works best with those who are alone. He can make us feel alone in a physical war, emotional war, or even a mental war. If we are alone, we will lose. This loss can result in either weakness or death, spiritually and (or) physically.

In 1 Corinthians 12, the apostle Paul describes the fellowship of the church as a human body. It might seem strange at first, but bear with him. Paul states, "Now you are the body of Christ, and each one of you is a part of it" (1 Corinthians 12:27). Without looking at the verses from a metaphoric point of view, it seems as if Paul was teaching an anatomy class. He speaks about eyes, hands, feet, and so on, telling us that we are one body of believers. By breaking it down, we can see that Paul is trying to tell us that, as Christians, we need to band together and become the body of the church. We must use our unique gifts, such as how an eye can see or an ear can hear, to further the kingdom. Paul tells us that through fellowship and bonding together, we can better spread the Gospel. We are more effective if we come together to accomplish the will of God.

If one person goes out in ministry, he or she can reach out to some types of people but not others. Imagine a young, energetic person trying to reach out to an older, more reserved person. Or on a more serious level, someone who has both parents trying to evangelize someone whose parents are dead or divorced. Everyone is different and needs to be reached differently. I am not neglecting to mention the power of God. He created the world and has the power to use anyone for anything. I am simply stating that He gifts people differently to be more effective for His kingdom. He wants us to work together, relying on one another, to create fellowship. Basically, the Bible tells us that by uniting with other Christians in fellowship, we can both defend and strengthen ourselves during the fight as well as spread the Good News of Jesus's resurrection more efficiently.

Acts 20:7 conveys much about fellowship, but it also describes a specific setting. Let's return, for a moment, to that third-story room. The believers are sitting, gathered around Paul, as he repeats the words Jesus once spoke while breaking bread and pouring wine. But what does communion have to do with fellowship?

Communion was first done at the last supper by Jesus before He went to die on the cross. Jesus warned His disciples about His impending death. He broke bread, demonstrating how His body would be broken for them, and poured wine, symbolizing the blood He would shed for all humankind. This was and still is a powerful symbol of His sacrifice. In a Christian fellowship setting, this symbol is important and not only encourages but also helps everyone involved to remember Jesus's sacrificial love. Jesus Himself said, "Do this (communion) in remembrance of me" (Luke 22:19).

Going back to the idea of a battlefield, imagine the lone warrior suddenly now surrounded by other warriors. They begin a battle cry and beat their shields. They yell out the name of their country and chant. Whatever they are doing, they are doing it to signify who they are and who or what they are fighting for. In our case, it's the memory of Christ's death and resurrection. We have a warrior rally: communion. The powerful idea that someone else went before us, suffered as we do, and then triumphed (like we will) helps bring us hope. Communion also strengthens our relationships with one another and binds us together. Through this action, we are reminded that we have a common goal and are unified under one Savior.

If we focus on the big picture, we will discover that God has created us to enjoy companionship. Adam had Eve. Paul was surrounded by fellow believers. We all need someone to encourage us. God gave us the gift of one another. Together we not only gain more hope but are also more effective in doing His will. God gifted us with communion to bring us together. This communion is our rally cry. Through His gifts of fellowship and communion, we can remember what we are fighting for: salvation and eternity as one body of believers.

CHAPTER 2

Sacrifice

Paul spoke to the people and, because he intended to leave the next day, kept on talking until midnight. There were many lamps in the upstairs room where we were meeting.

—Acts 20:7–8

In the last chapter, we studied fellowship, examining how Paul and the disciples were celebrating communion together. Continuing in that idea, we get to verses 7 and 8. Paul continues to speak, share communion, and teach the believers until midnight. Many people today would be sleeping by twelve o'clock in the morning, resting their eyes and dozing for work or school the next day. Paul wasn't focused on sleeping; he knew he was needed. And if you were doubting, he did have work the next day. Paul was going to be traveling.

Paul's call from Christ took him all over the early world to deliver the message of salvation. Many of his letters, now New Testament books, are named after the place or people he was ministering to. Paul went to Ephesus (Ephesians), Philippi (Philippians), Galatia (Galatians), Corinth (1 and 2 Corinthians), and Thessalonica (1 and 2 Thessalonians), to name a few. Even with the unadvanced transportation they had, Paul was constantly traveling. These modes of transportation did not make the task easy. Traveling was time-consuming and painstaking work! Paul was about to travel the next day to Assos (in Turkey), yet he was so devoted to the believers that he chose preaching over sleeping. Instead of fulfilling his own needs, Paul served and sacrificed without quitting, continuing to speak the message to the Ephesian people.

We can also observe that the people themselves stayed there until midnight. How would you like to go to church earlier in the day and listen to the pastor preach throughout the night? Not many people would be able to or want to do this. Sometimes a one-hour sermon is enough to make us drowsy. Yet the hearts of these early Christians were open to the message, yearning for it so badly that they sacrificed sleep to hear it. Like Paul, many of the people listening probably had things to do the next day, yet they paused what they were doing to continue to learn and fellowship. What did both Paul and the listeners do to gain more spiritual strength? They both had to make a sacrifice.

Sacrifices are extremely significant in the Bible, and the meaning is drastically different in the Old Testament in comparison to that of the New Testament. In the Old Testament, sacrifices were made to help cleanse the Israelites. Following God's commands and laws, His people would slaughter an animal, burning up certain parts of it, to ask God for forgiveness. This may seem strange to those in the twenty-first century, but for the Israelites, it was symbolic of God's forgiveness and their release from death in sin. Sacrifices were a part of worship to God, yet some people used the sacrifices incorrectly. To correctly offer a sacrifice, the Israelite had to get the best of what he had and present it to the Lord. The story of Cain and Abel illustrates what types of sacrifices God is pleased with and what types of sacrifices He despises (Genesis 4:7).

Cain and Abel are the children of Adam and Eve, who were mentioned previously. The story tells of Cain giving his leftovers to God but Abel giving the first of his flock. In the end, Cain ends up killing Abel out of jealousy, as God was more pleased with the sacrifice Abel presented. Before the murder, God warned Cain, "If you do what is right, will you not be accepted?" (Genesis 4:7a). God wanted Cain to give his first and best of what he had.

Later on, in the Old Testament, the Israelites celebrated a holiday called First Fruits. During this holiday, the people would collectively sacrifice the best of what they had and present it to the Lord. God deserves the first and best of all that we have. It should be noted that the Old Testament sacrifices and ideas were centered around physical work. You had to watch over your animals or plant, harvest, and care for your crops. It took a lot of toiling and sweat to get even the smallest items to sacrifice. Yet in the end, God blessed those who willingly sacrificed their earnings to Him, giving them immense blessings in return.

The New Testament, however, has a very different definition of sacrifice. Being the greatest example of sacrifice of all time, Jesus Christ sacrificed His perfect life in heaven to come down to earth, a place of imperfection and sin. He sacrificed His time by teaching and sacrificed His power by healing. In an ultimate act of love, Jesus sacrificed his life and died a sinner's death. This took no effort upon our part, whereas Old Testament sacrifices required us, as humans, to give to God through our own works. The New Testament form of sacrifice is an example of God giving to us through His grace. God knew that humanity was incapable of earning salvation on their own. Salvation is far too complicated and lofty for us to attain, let alone understand. So, God sent down Jesus, a man adept of bearing that load, to make a way for us to receive salvation. Death was inevitable, but through the freedom from sin that Jesus brought, we can now live for Him. Similarly to Old Testament sacrifices, a blessing results from Jesus's sacrifice. With God, there are no sacrifices without blessings. Jesus Christ, being the first sacrifice, received a blessing: the first gift of eternal life. We, as His children and heirs, will also be given eternal life through what He has done. But even before that, He has given us the gift of the Holy Spirit. The Spirit will act as a mentor to guide us until Christ's return. We are endlessly blessed!

How do we inherit this blessing? Who is eligible? Jesus just asks one thing from those who seek it. It does not require work or action on our part. It only comes with a sacrifice—a small sacrifice on our part that pales in comparison to His blessings for us. We don't have to work by planting crops or watching over animals. In fact, all we have to do is give up! We must sacrifice our self-centeredness, allowing Jesus to take control. We don't have to toil like the men in the Israelite camp. We just have to submit and sacrifice our lives to Him. I know that I feel more comfortable having the Creator of the universe, Who knows past, present, and future, guide me through this life. Many times, I do not know what I am going to do throughout the week, while God knows the very number of hairs on my head! To receive this gift, all it takes is a sacrifice of control. God will take pleasure in guiding you in the paths of righteousness.

So, what place does sacrifice have within the modern culture? You may have not sacrificed your life to Christ yet. If you have not, I strongly recommend you do! I believed that my life was running smoothly while I was in control, but after hard times came, I realized that I was walking a path of destruction. When I finally gave up, God revealed things to me that I had never thought about, giving me a whole new hope and perspective. When I sacrificed my life to Him, it wasn't a mere prayer; it was letting go of life as I knew it, letting God take the reins.

So, what if you are saved, and you have already sacrificed your life to Christ? I'm sorry, but I will never believe you if you tell me that you have done so. I say this because this sacrifice is not a once-in-a-lifetime experience but an everyday habit! One animal sacrifice was not suitable for the Israelites, nor is making one decision enough for us. God gives us small opportunities throughout the day to sacrifice to Him, and we must choose to give Him our first. God tells us to live life His way, not because He wants or needs the respect (even though He does deserve it) but because He wants us to conduct ourselves as Jesus did. Life is easier and safer when He is in the lead. True life comes when God has asked us to sacrifice our sins of greed, lust, hate, lying, and so on to Him, and we obey.

What sacrifices does God specifically want from us?

The first sacrifice is to let God take the lead, allowing Him to guide your life and lead it in the way He wants it to go. After you have submitted to Him, He asks that we make small Holy Spirit–driven sacrifices on a daily basis. Whether it is saving money when we desire to spend it, using our time wisely, or keeping from sleep to preach the Gospel, God wants us to be open to sacrifice. What is He calling you to sacrifice? Keep in mind that after the sacrifice, God richly blesses.

CHAPTER 3

Spiritual Boredom

Seated in a window was a young man
named Eutychus, who was sinking into a
deep sleep as Paul talked on and on.

—Acts 20:9a

Meetings can be boring. School can be boring. Life itself can be boring. All humans experience the feeling at one time or another. Human beings yearn for action and adventure and constant stimulation to keep them from this dreaded boredom. Within Acts 20:9, we find a bored young man named Eutychus. We are uncertain about Eutychus's life, as he is only mentioned once in the Bible. Nevertheless, his testimony is in the scriptures.

If we think back over the past few verses of Acts 20, we can recall that the early Christians were fellowshipping and sharing God's love with one another. It was late at night, or early morning, and the men and women did not cease to worship even at such late hours. These people were devoted, motivated, and focused. When reading the Bible, I find myself feeling a sense of failure when I compare myself to the spiritual heroes depicted in its pages. Yet the Bible is truth and speaks truth, conveying a real story about real events. Such is the case with Eutychus's story.

Returning to the idea of the gathered Christians, Eutychus was inside the room praising with those around him. Paul had begun to speak, and Eutychus chose to sit down in a surprising location. Eutychus sat on a windowsill. The fact that he was sitting in a window may be astounding enough, especially since the gathering was on the third story. More importantly, Eutychus began to fall asleep, into a "deep sleep," while in the window. You don't want to ever sit in a windowsill, especially if you are drifting off! Both facts are concerning, though it is not the physical position but rather the mental position that is alarming.

Sometimes in life, we find ourselves kneeling to God, praying earnestly for ourselves and others, yet we are bored. We read the Bible and go to church but feel bored. We can be fellowshipping and listening to an apostle preach, yet we can still be bored. It's not the physical position of reading a Bible, praying, talking, teaching, or doing good that keeps you moving forward. It is our mental position that makes or breaks our faith. Staying focused and motivated comes from maintaining a Christ-centered mentality, constantly pressing on to "run with perseverance the race marked out for us" (Hebrews 12:1). This principle is difficult to truly grasp, yet it makes a difference in your life once you obey it. Compare this to brushing your teeth. The first time you brushed your teeth as a child, you loved the idea of it. Everything from the brushing sounds to the taste of toothpaste fascinated you. But now that you are older, having brushed your teeth hundreds of times (I hope), it is not quite as interesting. In fact, some nights you may not want to brush your teeth. You still do it because you must, going through the motions to keep yourself healthy, but you do not have a brush-your-teeth-because-you-love-it-so-much mentality. The Christian faith is the same way.

When you first become a Christian, your life is turned around. You are excited about every aspect of it, and you want to do everything you can to possess such joy. But sadly, like the toothbrushing example, it can get boring and feel like a chore. Spiritual boredom happens to everyone, tempting them to quit or give up on their faith altogether. This spiritual issue develops when we become tired of keeping from sin. It is difficult to do the right thing, especially when the wrong thing seems more enjoyable. Yet Paul said to "never be lacking in zeal" and to "keep your spiritual fervor, serving the Lord" (Romans 12:11). Living life the way God desires goes against our human nature and can cause us to become tired or bored if we neglect to possess the right mentality.

Eutychus was an adult, most likely able to still sit on the windowsill physically. But like I mentioned, it wasn't the physical position but the mental position that created problems. Eutychus probably thought he needed sleep, much like we think we need the fulfilling feeling of sin. He slowly fell asleep, just as Christians slowly fall back into their sinful habits. The temptation was pressing, and Eutychus gave in. We, as Christians, are weak, constantly being tempted to fall back into sin. Yet Jesus, giving us hope and showing us that it is possible, made a way for us to fight that urge. Jesus Himself stated, "In this world you will have trouble. But take heart! I have overcome the world" (John 16:33). Notice how Jesus knew we would have trouble. He warned against spiritual boredom and the desire to give up on the faith. Jesus adds encouragement after this warning. He has overcome it already! Through Him, His strength and example, we can overcome. This is the right mentality to have when facing times of spiritual boredom.

Christians can also feel bored because we know we are unable to resist. It seems pointless. Paul states, "For I do not do the good I want to do, but the evil I do not want to do-this I keep on doing" (Romans 7:19). Even Paul, a man who had seen Jesus personally, had spiritual troubles and failures. But when we see how Jesus overcame sin as a man, "pressing on" to eternity, we can regain hope. When we get bored with faith, feeling like our hearts and minds are stagnant, persistently aiming toward sin, we can continue and take hope in Christ. Even in the midst of our struggle, we receive encouragement to press on. When spiritual boredom arises, I advise you to set aside time to pray and petition with God. He knows how hard it is to resist sin. Jesus was tempted many times while He was here on earth. When Jesus was tired, He asked God for strength. We should do the same. When our mentality is Christ focused and our first desire is to draw nearer to God, He will help us overcome boredom and sinfulness. Call on Him in your struggle, and He will rescue you from even the deepest sins. "God is faithful; He will not let you be tempted beyond what you can bear" (1 Corinthians 10:13).

We have reviewed how mental/spiritual boredom brought Eutychus to boredom, but what about his physical positioning? Even though the physical position that Eutychus was in was not necessarily concerning, it still contributed to his ultimate demise. Eutychus never would have fallen asleep in the window if he had never been in the window in the first place. On top of struggling against sin, being in the wrong place at the wrong time can contribute to boredom.

I mentioned the body of Christ in the first chapter of this book. Let's return to that idea. Ephesians 4: 11-13 states, "Christ himself gave the apostles, the prophets, the evangelists, the pastors and teachers, to equip his people for works of service, so that the body of Christ may be built up until we all reach unity in the faith and in the knowledge of the Son of God and become mature, attaining to the whole measure of the fullness of Christ." As I have previously discussed, we all belong to this metaphoric body of Christ. God designed each person to be a separate part of it and to accomplish their respective duties. But what if someone who God designed to be a pastor becomes a greeter? Boredom. What about a worship leader working as an usher? Boredom.

Many times, boredom occurs when we are out of place within the body of believers, when we are doing something we were not created to do. This is when sin gets its hold on us and the devil begins to whisper in our ears. It would be difficult to be a scientist when you studied theatre. Or a mathematician when you majored in English. It is the same within the body of Christ. It is impossible to stay focused on the track God has set you on when you are *not on* the track He wants you on. God will lead you to the things He wants you to do; you just have to trust Him.

Sometimes it is necessary for us to make sacrifices for the body of believers, serving in places we feel inadequate or misplaced. But this itself is part of God's plan and requires clear guidance from God.

Discovering the place in which God wants you to serve comes with spending time with Him. Taking a moment to speak with God will both free you from your boredom and make visible the path He created for you.

Boredom comes when you are out of place physically and mentally. Spiritual boredom follows those same guidelines. Jesus warned us to fight against this boredom (which will inevitably come) and to rely on Him. Look over your life and ask yourself if you are bored in your faith. If so, ask God to show you what you need to change, petitioning Him to redirect your path to match up with His. God will give you the strength to do what He asks you to accomplish.

CHAPTER 4

Future Focus

When he was sound asleep, he fell to the ground
from the third story and was picked up dead.

—Acts 20:9b

Spiritual boredom is not a thing to mess with. When I was young, I thought that life would just persist as usual. I'd eventually grow up, finish school, get married, have kids, and die similarly to everyone else. My mom was still alive, my dad was still alive, and my brother and sister were still alive. In my little mind, people lived a very long time. I thought that accepting Jesus could be done later because I would have a lifetime to make that decision. I could accept Him when I finished school and the pressures subsided. I could accept Him when I got married (and say two different "I do" statements). I could even accept Him while on my deathbed, living as I wanted until the day I perished. But as I matured, my thoughts changed.

Life is not long and sweet like we desire it to be.

Thousands die every day. Sickness runs wild. Death is a very common thing. I was shocked. I immediately rethought life. I came to the realization that time on earth is limited. That's when I had a mental shift. If life is so short, why have "fun" living in sin when the next day I could die? Why would I invest everything in something temporal when I could focus on eternity? This dilemma I had reminds me of the ever-popular marshmallow test.

The test begins with sitting children down by themselves in front of a marshmallow. The test issuer then tells the child to patiently wait to eat the marshmallow. If the subject waits, they are rewarded by receiving a second marshmallow. The child could choose patience, leading to a gain of two marshmallows, or they could choose immediate gratification, receiving one. The test commences with the child waiting in agony for minutes. It's quite amusing to watch the children squirm and wiggle their way through the short wait. Some children emerge successful, while others fail miserably within the first few seconds.

Life is similar to this marshmallow test. Time on earth is extremely short, just like the minutes of waiting for the children. I now ask you, why eat the one marshmallow when you could wait for a much better reward? Heaven is more than double our earthly pleasures. It is similar to an eternal flow of marshmallows, everything we'd ever desire and all the pleasures in the world, without consequences (or calories). I bring this up because Eutychus had the same mentality as we do, wanting the here and now, unable to resist the temptation that was so enticing. He couldn't resist sleep, as we learned in the last chapter. What was his consequence? Death.

In multiple places, the Bible calls death "sleep." In our case, if we don't resist sin, what's our consequence? Death. Other than the reference to marshmallows, this chapter has been very negative but important nonetheless. Perhaps Francis Chan explained our time on earth most effectively.

In one of his presentations, Chan used a lengthy rope to demonstrate the time line of life. On the end he held was a small piece of red tape. It was roughly three to five inches long, representing our life on earth. After telling his audience to suppose the other end of the rope (which was several feet long) went on forever, Chan explained that life is brief in relation to eternity. When I began to truly understand how short life is, the reality of how long eternity will be became apparent.

When we think about eternity, it's hard to even begin to comprehend what it truly entails. If you go to heaven, the pleasure will last an eternity. If you go to hell, the torture will last an eternity. Eternity is eternity. Heaven will be wonderful, filled with only the most perfect, pure, and holy elements. It is direct life in the presence of God. It's bound to be astounding! But that's just one end of the spectrum. At the other end is a complete separation from God. That means agony, suffering, anguish, torment, and terrifying aspects we are incapable of fathoming. Sadly, this is where we are all bound to go. We were all born with a one-way ticket. Romans 3:23 states it clearly, "for all have sinned and fall short of the glory of God." Luckily, Jesus came and, as discussed in the preceding chapters, released us from this bondage. It's now our choice to accept the return ticket or continue on the literal path to hell, where there will be no release.

Jesus is our Savior, the key to eternal life. Notice that the first portion of Acts 20:9 stated that Eutychus "was sinking into a deep sleep." He had not yet reached that life-changing moment when he careened out of the window. But in the last part of the verse, it reads "he was sound asleep." Notice the shift. He was sinking, but then he sunk. Do not worry! No matter how far you are, as long as you still have breath in your lungs and a beating heart, it is never too late. Life is a sinking ship. You choose to get on the lifeboat or not. We must make the right decision to save ourselves and begin our eternity with our Father. Continuing in sin is like going back to the sinking ship or, as the Bible states, like a dog returning to its vomit (Proverbs 26:11). Obviously, no one wants to go to a place of vile evil, a place exceedingly worse than a sinking ship or vomit.

Salvation requires us to think ahead and be future focused. When I say *think ahead*, I am not indicating worry about what is coming. Jesus Himself said, "Therefore do not worry about tomorrow, for tomorrow will worry about itself. Each day has enough trouble of its own" (Matthew 6:34). When I say *future focused*, I mean the very opposite of worrying about what is to come. Living future focused is living life keeping your eyes on heaven, neglecting to worry about the here and now but rather looking toward the approaching day. Living future focused is waiting patiently for that new marshmallow, resisting the temporal one in front of you. Even though this life may have unending troubles, heaven is our safe haven. Paul states very often in his writings that he is running the race with his eyes on the prize (1 Corinthians 9:24; 2 Timothy 4:7; Hebrews 12:1). That prize is much more than a gold medal (in fact,

Revelation 21:21 states that the very streets of heaven will be gold).

This is what we should do so we turn our sinking into living: stay focused on eternity. And this is not just staying afloat; it's living in satisfaction through Christ Jesus. It is similar to getting off of your life raft and onto a yacht; an experience unlike any other. Reflecting on my days as a child, I recall asking God to teach me to think about my actions, before doing them, and how they would affect the future. Since then, I have been looking at things through a whole new lens, and God has helped me stay future focused in every aspect of life.

I invite you to join me in this future-focused, God-centered state of mind. We can embrace this new living by sharing the Gospel, fellowshipping, sacrificing, and living for God. He will guide us away from the sinking ship of human nature and lead us toward new life directed by His mighty hand.

CHAPTER 5

Unconditional Love

Paul went down, threw himself on the young
man and put his arms around him. "Don't
be alarmed," he said. "He's alive!"

—Acts 20:10

Recall the first chapter of this book. Think back to the idea
of an army on both sides of a battlefield. This concept is
coming back in verse 10 but in a slightly different manner.
Instead of talking about fellowship, let's shift our gaze to the
foundation of *all* fellowship, friendship, marriages, family,
and life itself: love. The story has progressed rapidly, and
within only two verses, the main character is introduced and
then dies. What began as a pleasant evening, to worship God
and enjoy one another, ended in great tragedy. Eutychus was
there one minute, gone the next. Even though this night is
akin to a horror movie, in verse 10, love is revealed.

There are two different kinds of love, conditional and
unconditional. Conditional love is the most common and

most destructive. It loves only if something is given in return. If nothing is given in exchange, the love fails, folding in on itself.

On the other end of the spectrum is unconditional love. This love has no prerequisites or expectations. Unconditional love can only come from God, and its greatest display is seen in the person of Jesus. Where conditional love would reject any form of suffering for the benefit of haters, unconditional love would die for its enemies. This love is so good, seemingly unrealistic and contradictory to the human nature of looking out for oneself. For humans, this love *is* unrealistic. For God, the Author of love, it is natural to display it constantly.

Whether you are His enemy or a committed Christian, you fall under God's amazing love. In fact, His love is so amazing that the human mind can't even begin to understand it. It's something so outlandish, so obscure, it seems as if there would be a lofty price to pay for it. But God's love, being unconditional, is easily found and demands no price. In fact, you are not required to love God in return to have Him love you. However, God's love cannot be truly experienced and enjoyed in a one-way relationship. Once you choose to love God, actioning your end of the relationship, amazing things happen. Instead of feeling lonely, you have a Friend. Instead of feeling oppressed, you stand unashamed. Instead of being confused, you can look forward to what lies ahead.

One of the benefits of this relationship with God comes in the form of a gift. He gives you the ability to give out unconditional love. Those who experience His love within them experience the shift from conditional to unconditional.

Like a name-brand shirt, this gift shows the Maker and Designer of this new love that clothes you. Jesus said, "By this everyone will know that you are my disciples, if you love one another" (John 13:35). Jesus is not referring to conditional love but unconditional love. This ties in with the idea of fellowship, a gathering of Christians to share in the unconditional love of the Lord.

What does all of this have to do with a (now) dead man? How could we possibly reference love when this story seems to be empty of it? If we return to the passage, verse 9 states that Eutychus fell from the third story and onto the ground. I must refrain from being overly graphic, but this incident was bound to be bloody. A fall like this would break bones, cause internal bleeding, and (like in this case) kill the victim. This whole situation was unlovely, yet amazing love emerges from it.

In response to Eutychus's fall, Paul (most likely accompanied by everyone else) ran down to see what had become of his friend. The dead man lay there, and Paul was moved with unconditional love. I am unsure of what I would do in this situation, but I am sure that I would not have reacted as Paul did. Verse 10 chronicles that Paul came down and threw himself on Eutychus, placing his arms around him. If this is not unconditional love, I do not know what is! Eutychus was not only in critical condition but a bloody, broken, obliterated condition. Yet Paul's unconditional love overlooked his friend's position, causing him to literally "throw himself" on the young man.

This is the type of love God has called us to enact. He sent Jesus Christ to earth, allowing Him to become part of the imperfect, chaotic mess that is humanity. Born in the most undignified way, the Son of God began His life of servitude. Constantly displaying unconditional love, Jesus was brought to the point where it killed Him. But in the end, in the best plot twist, God raised Jesus from the grave through this unconditional love. Much like Eutychus, Jesus was bloody, broken, and obliterated, yet God reached down, wrapped His arms around His Son, and raised Him back to life. Jesus was not the only human whom God chose to save. We are foul, bloodthirsty sinners at heart. We were not only going to experience physical death, but our spirits were already dead. Yet God had not accomplished His will in us. He did not want our lives to end in sin. Though we brought our demise upon ourselves (by falling asleep to His law), we were redeemed. Romans 5:8 states this idea better than I could ever put it, "But God demonstrates his own love for us in this: While we were still sinners, Christ died for us."

At the end of verse 10, God works through Paul to enact a miracle. Paul proclaims Eutychus alive, much like God proclaims us alive. What an amazing act of unconditional love He has done for us! Since we were given such an amazing gift, God has asked us to share it with others. You may know someone who is bloody and broken. Someone whose life is unlovely and messy. Someone who needs a friend to come and give them encouragement and the love they desperately need. Our flesh tells us to not to become involved in the affair; our conditional love shuns the idea of going near such a person. Yet the love that God has given us, the unconditional love of the Father, causes us to run to our neighbor and throw ourselves on them in compassion. Sharing this love is what God has called us to do and, like Paul, you could bring someone to life.

CHAPTER 6

Worship

Then he went upstairs again and broke bread and ate.

—Acts 20:11

Acts 20:7–12 demonstrates how God can use anything and will use anything wicked and damaging to further His kingdom. Imagine being a witness of this event. Maybe you were a close friend of Eutychus, or maybe you had just seen him in passing. Either way, you would have been shaken to the core if you watched him hurdle toward the ground from the third-story window. You would run down to the first floor in horror and shock to see the young man motionless. A chill would shoot down your spine. Your heart would break. Soon you would observe Paul run down and plead with God on behalf of Eutychus. He would throw himself on the man, and you would watch impatiently to see what God would do.

Sometimes life plays out much like this event did. You are confronted with something too big for you, something too difficult to handle, and you stand watching to see what God will do. Unfortunately, most times we are unsure of what will happen. We do not fully trust that God will act, yet we do not fully disbelieve in His mighty power. So we sit and wait in faith. Then, when all hope seems lost, God chooses to do something miraculous. When Abraham and Sarah were too old to have children, God gave them Isaac. When the Israelites lost hope in the desert, God split the sea. When Daniel was face-to-face with a ferocious den of lions, God shut the mouths of the beasts. When all humanity was lost, God sent down a Deliverer.

Many times, throughout the Bible and in our own lives, we are witnesses to the amazing power of God and His plans. God's ways are higher than our ways, and His thoughts are higher than our thoughts (Isaiah 55:9). In this particular story, when all was seemingly lost, a breath was heard from the mouth of Eutychus. He stood erect and saw the faces of those who had observed the whole scenario. Eutychus's heart beat faster with every renewed moment as he watched the men and women surrounding him praise the Lord. When God does something miraculous, we only have one response: worship.

It should be noted that the believers may or may not have played music on the night of Eutychus's fall. It is irrelevant, however, as worship is not a song, but an attitude of the heart. Worship is merely opening up your soul to acknowledge the power and greatness of the Lord. It is sacrificing your time in the here and now to focus on the goodness of the Creator. It is gathering with other believers to lift up the name of the Lord and express your gratitude for His unconditional love.

There are endless ways to praise the Creator, as He is endlessly creative. To get into a heart of worship, many different modes of praise can be actioned. Each of these unique forms of worship is not of our own doing but is yet another gift from God. It is such a special ability to be endowed with and is itself another reason to praise our Lord.

Though I will never be able to go through all of the methods of worship, I shall state some of the most common modes. Personally, I get into a worshipful heart through intellect. There is something so beautiful to me about the words in the Bible. I can sit, for hours on end, reading through its pages. Similarly, the sermon on a Sunday morning brings me into a heart of gratitude toward God. As I have found through experience and conversing with others, intellect is one of the least common modes of worship, yet it is still powerful.

Some people worship while in nature. For my mother, the most effective way to worship the Lord is to appreciate His greatness by adventuring into nature. As soon as she smells the flowers, watches a small squirrel pass by, and feels the cool breeze on her neck, her heart is filled with joy. It is the thought that the Lord, the Creator of the universe, has made all things so beautifully that sets her mind on His goodness. God created such intricate designs for us so we can see the power of His majesty before us.

Worship can also be achieved through music. This is possibly the most common way for people to get into a heart of worship. Christian songs themselves are often deemed "worship music." This is probably due to the intimacy of praising the Lord through a tune rather than words. Music is extremely powerful, and throughout the

Bible, this method of worship can be observed. Moses sang when he and the Israelites crossed through the waters on dry ground. Deborah sang when she and Barack fought back the opposing nations. David, the king of Israel, sang as a shepherd and continued to praise after he had been appointed to rule. This list could go on and on. Music is our creation of a tune, sung to the promises and goodness of our Creator.

Within the story of Eutychus, persistent worship is apparent. The people worshipped through intellect, while listening to Paul, and through remembrance, while partaking in communion. When all was brought to peace, the believers gathered to worship. This is important to remember because many times people cease to worship God when they are comfortable. When it is apparent that the objects of this life bring you dissatisfaction, it is natural to look to something bigger. When money is scarce, when possessions break down, and when troubles surround your thoughts, praising God is easy. But when you can enjoy the goodness of life around you, there seems to be no need to praise God. God is often forgotten when the things of this world become your god. But the things of earth are only temporary and are undeserving of our praise. It is imperative to remember to worship God during all circumstances of life.

Approaching Eutychus after he fell out of the window, Paul continued to worship. Paul knew the power of the Lord could save, and it was through this act of worship of that Christ's power moved through him to heal Eutychus. Paul had faith that "the prayer of a righteous person is powerful and effective" (James 5:16), which ultimately led to Eutychus's resurrection.

Most importantly, after Eutychus was raised, the people remained in worship, walking upstairs to celebrate the power of God together. It might have been easy, in this situation, to forget the power of God and stay focused on what had occurred rather than Who had made it occur. Yet these devoted disciples continued on in their night of worship, using the situation as a testimony to the mighty power of Jesus's holy name.

What is interesting is that the people partook in communion once more after the event. They had just taken the bread and the cup moments before. Why did they feel the need to do it again? The answer is simple: Eutychus's resurrection reminded them of Christ's. Jesus had been with them in their hearts, minds, and spirits throughout the entirety of that late night. It was through the power of Jesus that they had gathered in the first place. It was the power of Jesus that had raised Eutychus from the dead. It was the same power that moved through the disciples that night that had released them from spiritual destruction. The believers were reminded that Jesus Christ had dominion over all death, physical as well as spiritual, and they were moved to worship Him.

In our lives, we may feel like there is no reason to worship. We may feel like God has abandoned us, leaving us to suffer on this earth alone. But let me reassure you, just as He was with the disciples on the evening of Eutychus's demise, He is with us and is moving in us even now. His greatness can be seen at every angle of life, no matter which way we turn. We shall never cease to have reasons to worship our God.

CHAPTER 7

Comfort

The people took the young man home
alive and were greatly comforted.

—Acts 20:12

This is the last chapter of this book, centered around the last
verse of this story. We have covered a multitude of topics,
but this last topic will aid you in recalling and actioning the
rest. This last chapter is going to examine comfort, a key
element of the Christian faith.

Before we look at comfort, I want you to cast out of your
mind the modern idea of physical comfort. The comfort that
I am referencing within this last chapter is spiritual comfort,
vastly different from physical comfort. Jesus Christ did not
come to earth and die to save us from that which makes us
uncomfortable physically but rather that which torments
us in spirit.

To take a deeper look at what comfort is, let us examine
the opposite of comfort. Its antonym is *discomfort*, meaning

that you feel the absence of comfort. You cannot experience discomfort without comfort, as you cannot have darkness without light or cold without warmth. There needs to be something good that is missing in order for its opposite to exist. Discomfort is felt when something, or Someone, is missing.

Those who are not in Christ constantly deal with spiritual discomfort. Humans search until death to receive comfort but can never truly obtain it. Life is difficult, uncomfortable, and chaotic. Humanity is constantly subject to suffering and pain. We long to find the answers to life's problems. We can dig deeper and deeper but never find what we are truly looking for. We can claim to have the answers, but in reality, we patch up our emptiness with false assumptions.

This hole within each of us is real and is the sole cause of our discomfort. Our souls can be filled with evil or filled with good. Either the pleasures of this world reign inside your soul, or God does. Matthew 6:24 states, "No one can serve two masters. Either you will hate the one and love the other, or you will be devoted to the one and despise the other." Our souls are never empty, but we feel empty depending on what we fill them with.

This principle is like choosing to eat candy or a complete meal. One will satisfy the hunger, while the other leaves you starving. No matter how much of the candy you eat, you will never become full. On the contrary, overconsumption of candy can make you rather sick. With a meal, your hunger becomes satisfied, and you regain strength. The things of this world will never pacify you. Much like the human body is not designed to eat pure sugar and artificial flavorings, the materialistic pleasures of this world are not what we were intended to intake. We are created to fill ourselves with the Lord. He is our portion. He is our prize. This is what will eternally satisfy our needs and bring us true comfort.

Now let's look at the definition of comfort itself. Comfort can be defined as "a state of physical ease and freedom from pain or constraint." Satan shackles us and binds us to our sins and our shame. Not only are we empty from holding on to temporal things, but we are slaves to our past and the evil that is so prevalent within our lives. Those shackles weigh us down and keep us from experiencing the full comfort of God. We are unable to be comfortable when our chains are constantly rubbing against us, reminding us of our transgressions in the sight of God.

When Jesus Christ died, our shackles were shaken loose. Paul was imprisoned, with a fellow believer named Silas, for rebuking a spirit. After praising the Lord, a violent earthquake shook the chains off of their wrists, and they became free. If God can do mighty acts physically, how much more authority does He have to do this spiritually! The psalmist of Psalm 116 states, "Lord ... you have freed me from my chains" (Psalm 116:16). It was through the death of Jesus that our chains were finally broken.

God's comfort is unique. Though His comfort is not always physical, its spiritual prominence spills into our physical lives, allowing us to handle our problems with renewed peace. When we are faced with people who mistreat and accuse us, we can remember that "we are more than conquerors through him who loved us" (Romans 8:37). When we are struggling due to a lack of materialistic items, God's comfort allows us "to be content whatever the circumstances" (Philippians 4:11). This comfort is so great that in the midst of troubles, we can hold our heads up confidently and regain the strength to move forward.

If we return to the account in Acts, Eutychus had just been revived, and the believers once more worshiped the Lord. After this, verse 12 records that the believers were "greatly comforted." This means their voids were filled. They had been discomforted with the things of this world, as life is hard and painful. The believers were gathering together in discomfort, and God brought down His comfort in a surprising way. He filled the void through a demonstration of His power, causing a great spiritual freedom within His people.

As demonstrated in Acts 20:7-12, the most profound assurance we have is that Jesus Christ brings us comfort from the fear of death. The end always induces fear and sadness, yet His comfort overcomes this. When the power of God was displayed in Eutychus's revival, the believers regained hope in Jesus's death-conquering name. They were reminded that all sin and evil had been conquered, and that the struggles of this life had been pacified by the overwhelming greatness of God. We must live in remembrance of this, keeping hope that we will not meet a dead-end demise. Rather, we should remember that our graves are only a temporary place, and we will one day be reunited with our heavenly Father.

This book is coming to an end, yet I pray that its purpose shall endure. I hope that you will meditate on each chapter of this book. Following the concepts contained within will be difficult, and I myself have never and will never master them. But I assure you that with the comfort of God, you will be filled and prepared to pour out. No longer will it be such a daunting task to fellowship and sacrifice. It will not be as difficult to refrain from spiritual boredom or keep focused on the eternal. You will find yourself able to love unconditionally and worship fully. God gives us His overflowing comfort to meet our basic needs and then continues to bless us with more. We will never feel empty when we are filled with His freedom, when we are set free to accomplish His will.

ACKNOWLEDGMENTS

I thank my God every time I remember you.

—Philippians 1:3

First and foremost, I want to thank God for using me, an imperfect human being, as a megaphone for His message. I am in awe with all You have done in and through my life.

To my mom, for being so supportive of my goals for this book and for representing me throughout the publishing process. I am grateful for all the hours you have spent editing this book, encouraging me to finish what I started.

To my dad, for guiding me in my spirituality and teaching me about Jesus Christ. You have always been (and will always be) my role model.

To Rachel Jolin, for being an inspiration to me and for encouraging me to write. All of your prayers and suggestions have been extremely beneficial throughout the writing process.

To the Corliss family, for being an example of Christian fellowship/family to me. I am grateful that God has put you in my life.

To all my pastors and youth group leaders that have

supported me over the years and instilled the Word of God in me.

To my Christian brothers and sisters, for encouraging me and walking in faith.

To the apostle Paul, for being obedient to God by spreading the message of Jesus Christ to the Gentiles throughout the world.

To Eutychus, whom God used to convey the message of this book.

To everyone who has supported me in prayer. Look at what God has brought into fruition! Please continue praying that God will reveal Himself to the readers of this book.

To everyone who has supported me financially: Tony Albright, Mariel Barreras, Steve Barry, Erika Cianciulli, Mark and Mandi Corliss, Rich Davis, Mike, Chris and Joe DeRienzo, Richard DeRienzo, Joey and Bonnie Gregory, Rebekah and Curtis Gump, Thomas Helms, Chandler Hughes, Bryan Kole, Hollie Lind, Ashley Mann, Randy Merkes, Georgie Morrison, Colleen Pak, Lisa Ricco, Lacy Richardson, Teresa Salgado, Emma Shaul, Andrea Todd, Marlene Trzaska, Cal and Natalie Walters, Erica Yoon, Becky Zaloudek, and all of those who gave anonymously.

And finally, to my readers, for being open to the message of this book. Throughout every step of the writing and publishing process, I have had you in mind. God bless you!

BIBLIOGRAPHY

Holy Bible: New International Version. Michigan: Zondervan, 2011. Print.

Crazy Love. "Francis Chan: Living Eternally (The Rope Sermon)." *YouTube*, 4 Dec. 2014, https://www.youtube.com/watch?v=bfvbH4Ugj7M.

"Comfort: Definition of Comfort by Lexico." *Lexico Dictionaries | English*, Lexico Dictionaries, https://www.lexico.com/en/definition/comfort.

Printed in the United States
By Bookmasters